Mime Musings

Mime Musings

Charles Cozart

iUniverse, Inc.
Bloomington

Mime Musings

iUniverse books may be ordered through booksellers or by contacting:

iUniverse
1663 Liberty Drive
Bloomington, IN 47403
www.iuniverse.com
1-800-Authors (1-800-288-4677)

ISBN: 978-1-4759-5800-3 (sc)
ISBN: 978-1-4759-5801-0 (ebk)

Printed in the United States of America

iUniverse rev. date: 10/23/2012

<u>Credits</u>

Mime Musings

By

Charles Cozart

Author of

Tales From an Abnormal Reality

Illustrations by

Jarrod Lucero

Published by

iUniverse Publishing

This book is dedicated to all the characters, both real and imaginary, who have come together to inspire these Mime Musings.

<u>Introduction</u>

Words paint pictures. Within the pages of Mime Musings, the figurative language of imagination paints with the brace brush stroked of light pastel, but they are drawn down with thin lines of color. Hopefully, they ride to a crescendo of sight, then move to a staccato of sound, and finally drop a Diminuendo of vision, I have appealed to your senses. What do you see? What do you hear? What do you taste? What do you smell? What do you feel?

Ad you lie back in the sweet grass, can you see the faces of clowns in "Clouds and Clowns"? Can you hear the click-clack and rumble in "Hobo Journey"? Can you taste the sweet juicy Hackberries, turning black on the bush in "Hackberry Creek"? Can you smell the sweet fragrance of freshly mown hay in "April to October"? Can you feel that place, the very place, in "The Spot"?

With each line, each verse, each passage, I appeal to your memory and to your emotions. Some will make you laugh, some will make you cry. Some of these "scratching" will give you chill bumps, because you'll remember when you were there.

With each illustration, Jarrod Lucero has captured his interpretation of the meaning of each poem. However, those of you who read each line and view each images will create your own world. The real meanings that underlies each line and hides between the verses and images that have been created.

The meaning and emotion that you conjure up from these verses will come from the magic of the "Mime Musings" of your own mind.

Enjoy!!!

Thank you for reading.

Thank you for seeing.

Table of Contents

Lives

<u>Lives</u>

It's funny how lives

Are bound so tight

Spider web

In a holly bush.

Oh! How we strive

To tear them apart

But . . . the circles binds us tight

Like dream catcher in moonlight.

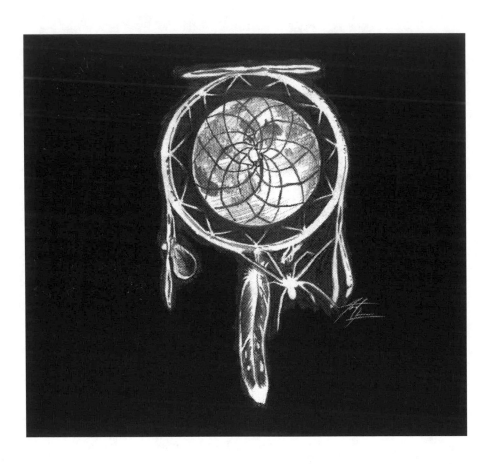

Hobo

Journey

Hobo Journey

He roamed dark forests

With spruces tall

Scanned both oceans

Watching breakers fall

Walked sandy fields

Hickory hoe in hands

Where snow-topped cotton

Waist high stands

But he's rather ride

Wheels of steel

North, South, East to West

Back and forth he'll feel

Chugging smoke

Diesel train

Iron on iron

Cranking music in his brain

Sun or rain

A box car joke

Bummin' for a winter coat

'neath trestle bridges

Sanctuary home

Long as there's life

And rails to roam

Crackers and a can of beans

Hobo jungle fires

Hot beer, hole-y jeans

Smiling faces, shared cigar

Mad Dog or Thunderbird

Tall tales from afar

When he arrives, he'll be there

Gleaming eyes wisdom to share

He'll not shirk from a suited stare

So with palm outstretched and pockets full

He'll hop a freight and go somewhere

Indian
Time

Indian Time

Days and night go fleeting by

Faster than a blinking eye

Seasons come and go so fast

Crating shadow visions of the past

A laugh, a cry

The seconds fly

Sunny days

Moonlight bright

Starry, starry night

Infinite memories

Take speeding flight

Flame upon a candle stick

Outshines the black of candle wick

Melting down the shrinking flame

Accentuates life's sweet, sweet perfume

Inside the vortex

We safely stay

Collecting pleasure from each day

With openness of eager eyes

Inside our heart we realize

With each previous breath

There's no finality

In captured tales

From an abnormal reality

Anywhere

Lost

World

<u>Anywhere Lost World</u>

An entire population hardy visible in the mind's eye

Like the thin rectangle sky

Trapped between rooftop lines

Emasculated by a million miles of concrete

Steel, glass and chrome

The color is gray, no opaque brilliance of horizon

No essence of sunrise or sunset

Just one constant thinness engulfing gray

In the shadowed darkness

Not to be seen writing tattered lines

Lyrics burned on brown paper bags, verses churned

Watching, listening to a blank faces of a city

On an endless merry-go-round

It is by reason and logic that

Hour by the hour we die

It is by reason and logic that hour by hour we die

It is by emotion and passion that we live

It is by imagination that into

The sun's rays, wings spread, we fly

Mental White Out

Mental White Out

In dark of night with

Lamps turned low

Shades pulled down

In candle glow

Wax slides down

The candle shaft

Last I walk, last I laugh

Caverns of my mind

Searching closets

Where I find

Doors ajar and shelves covered

With cobwebs and dust

Memory, a created myth

This, that and the other

Here and there I'll discover

All the things I've put away

Satisfied

I'll close the door and walk away

Sitting in a tree I think

The whole damn thing was just a blank

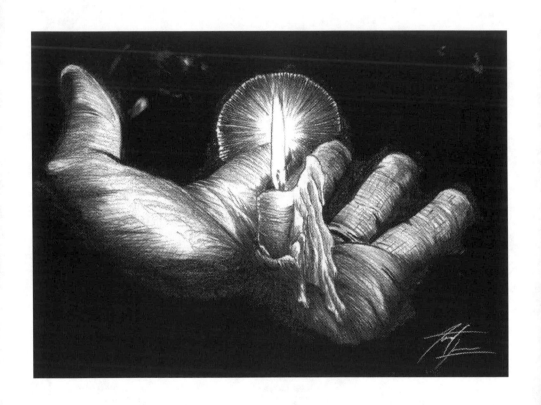

In My
Mind,
Maybe,
Maybe
Not

In My Mind, Maybe, Maybe Not

Clothes in a knapsack

By an unlocked door

In my mind maybe

Ready to leave forevermore

Highway men and hippies galore

Hoboes, beatniks

Street-painted whores

I've known them all

Who's keeping score . . .

Living days, living nights

Searching souls in full flight

Disrupts societies

Locked up fright.

Ready to accept

Or stand for a fight.

Concrete jungle glows

In street light

What a sight

Neon, purples, green, red

Blinking, flashing against your head

Street people moving, caught, held tight

Scratchings

<u>Scratchings</u>

After some thought

For some reason I cannot say

That reason has planned

Because the sequence of events

Have fallen upon me

By no hand of my own or

Any particular design that I can imagine

Or sign that I can recognize

That would cause the reason

By which I am so perplexed.

Though I can recognize

No real or tangible excursion

Into the realm of thought

A search for the reason of thought

Has begun.

Try as I may to put this thing

That I cannot describe away

The If of It has confounded me

And It has counted coup upon my senses.

When I am awakened into the

Consciousness of thought

The Invasion of It consumes me

As bindweed with its exquisite

Bloom and intoxicating aroma

Entraps prairie grasses

Presenting its exquisite beauty to the

Eye on the outside

But clogging the vision that lies underneath

It's confusing.

The search is leading

Through murky silt-infested waters

The depth of which is not marked

By clarity

And I am not convinced, at this point,

If there are guides

Who have enough power

To illuminate the path.

When I am asleep

Painted war ponies with

Flaring nostrils, flying manes

Eyes of flowing red, eagle feathers

Tied in their tails bring

Unrecognizable riders

To invade my dreams

Do experts have the answers

Not the ones I have asked.

And if there are experts

Apparently, at first sight

I cannot find them.

For the questions I have been asking myself

Only produce a cascade of questions

Creating a continuous flow if inquiry

Flowing into turbulent pool of answerlessness.

Could it be that the flood of questions

Is not designed to have answers.

Maybe the search for the answers

Holds only the key to the questions

Alas, again is such confusion

Only an ageless rhetoric???????

Or is it a mere excuse

To keep the questions simple

Letting single cell answers, the

Paramecium of mental cognizance

Evolve into the life form

Of smoke and mirrors of assumed knowledge

Calculated only as a defense mechanism

To disguise the real question

Confounding the search.

Even upon hard rock

The unshod pony leaves

The presence of its existence.

Possibly somewhere within infinity

A question leaves the presence of its answer

Hopefully this befuddlement is but

The beginning

A finding. Directing us to a hidden path

Or maybe not.

Maybe I am thinking

Therefore I am vulnerable to confusion.

OR IS IT

Mass confusion!!!!

And I am simply a production of It!

Blank Pages

Blank Pages

What is there about those times

Or time itself

When it is impossible to take a pen

And draw black lines

That paint pictures

Ever so delicately over white blankness

It is not amnesia or for lack of thought

As thought comes at you

From a kaleidoscope of chaos

I have poured myself

Through the cartridge of my pen

Time and time again

As I, the self-proclaimed wordsmith

Draw order from chaos

I look at the page

And it is blank

I close myself

And go into the night searching

It is possible, at times

That blankness is the only safety net

For sanity.

And sanity is by definition is order

Or blank lines placed meticulously

One after another

On pages that are blank.

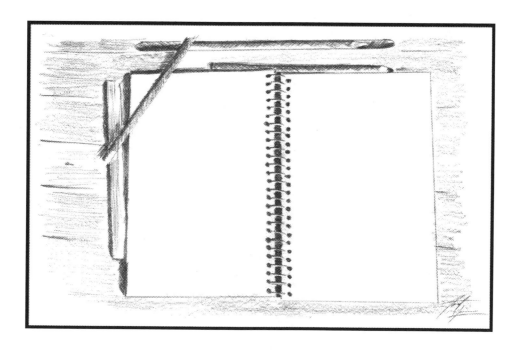

Farming with a One-Way

<u>Farming with a One-Way</u>

The frame's a whole lot rusty

Got some broken welds

Probably more like a few

Ol' thing ain't seen paint

Since 1942.

Disks are bent and chipped a bit

Plowin' hard ground

Bet I hit a rock or two

Tires are usually flatter than a fritter

New used ones we bought ain't much better

Marker wheels bent clean outta shape

Looks more like a big black grape

But with a pin hooked in the draw bar

It hugs the tractor tight

We'll knock out a few more acres

Before the sun goes down tonight

You know, wheat is getting' cheaper

Corn an' milo 'bout the same

But if the banker goes the loan

And God decides to let us stay

We'll keep a workin' this ol' land

At least for one more day

Though the weather could be better

Guess it's not as bad as that

Life is just like the sometimes

When you're farming . . . . with a one-way

The Spot

The Spot

Find a spot on the porch

Be still, oh be real still

Coyote calls

Spirit hawk to speak

A spot on the porch

Weather worn, knotted

Gnarled, calling

Where life penetrates

The essence of being

Move slowly, move searching

You'll find it consoling.

Be still

Oh, be real still

Re-open the doors

Relax into life

Then begin to drop

Crusty demons of dirt

One speck of sand at a time

Hourglass, revision

Our glass seeks vision

Stoned, immaculate

Rolling down the rim, accentuates

Cistern barrel full of rain

Fruit of tangled vine

Smokin' cheap Key Largo wine

Last days of rage, choking

Against the machine

Order cloistered

Choose whirling

Tornadic eradication of dreams

Not centered

Spilt milk, rancid butter

Whiskey down the edge of a crystal glass

Market to the soulless masses

Get the nuts together

Exhibit bare beginnings

Open road, open mind

Euphoric, erotic guidance

Listen

Find the Spot Behind

Be still, oh be real still

And penetrate

April
and
October

April and October

From a chair on the deck

Cold marker makes noise

With mighty puffs

Silver maples shake

Rattling from the north

Winter warriors, gird loins, and poise

To strike through oaks

Bitter and cold

Heavy laden, oxen yokes

Was a blink of an eye

A short time ago

We waited for spring, the girl and I

Waiting, wanting, expectantly

For the bloom of the wild rose bush

Coaxed from virgin green

By the shrill scream

Of a whippoorwill cry

A new love affair that left no scars

Ignited by constellations, moons, and stars

April and October, strange months of the year

Time exists but isn't clear

Not summer, not winter

Almost spring, almost fall . . . very queer.

Quail and deer tread on dry grass

While cloudy twilight casts

Shadows on the hill, such ghosts

And valleys fill with shrouded mist

Time travelers

Unravelers . . . seasons ring

Waiting for blossoms again

And the love affair of spring

spring stillness

<u>Spring Stillness</u>

In the stillness

There is a song

That night birds perch and sing

While on the creek

Lightning bugs dance a jig in spring

Blossoms on the prairie bloom

Before summer weaves

A heated loom

And life like a soft breeze

Is being still

And listening to the whippoorwill

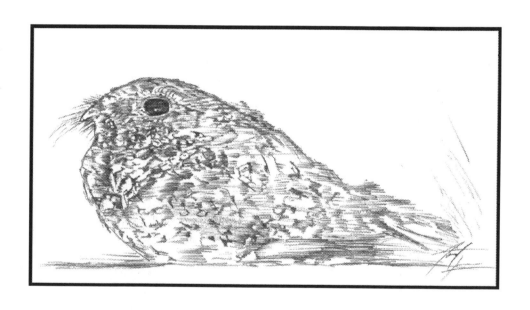

Dent de Lion

Dent de Lion

I shouldn't care if dandelions

Rise above the ground

Their fluffy mane all stringy

Their galaxy of space

Oblong and round

Syph's golden locks fall soft to earth

Slight breezes carry them to birth

Everywhere far and near

A dandelion roars

From Syph's tragic tear

In ancient times when Rome was king

And Greeks set forth their prose

The lowly dandelion was more erotic

To lovers

Than an orchid or a rose

Mimosa Madness

Mimosa Madness

I was sitting in the mimosa tree

Taking in a sinking sun

Remembering other days

Watching painted ponies run

Watching the world turn upside down

Spring plays a traveling sound

In the lines of the song I have found

There is no difference between

A bronc rider and a biker

Except an earring

Dangling in the breeze

Both are looking for a lighter moment

That'll put their life at ease

And a woman

They can call their friend

There is no difference between

A matador and a hobo

Cruising around the horn

Except a flowing red cloak

Or a whiskey-laced with coke

There's a never-ending broken white line

Shouting out there is not enough time

Bandanas flying in the wind

Sayin' come on

I know you

Want you to be

Here today and gone tomorrow

Share the bottle in this bag

We're all livin' lives of touch and tag

Traveling down another white line

To one more place

In another time

Motors rumbling in the cool night air

We engage the gear

Release the clutch

Sooner or later

We all get there

Hackberry Creek

Hackberry Creek

I sit in the shade of a cottonwood tree

My dog, my bro, my sis and me

Breeze painted leaves

Colors circling in a dance to see

Sun's shining bright

On the Hackberry Creek

Berries black

Ripe on the vine

Purple juices

A spider web

An orange sunshine

Leaned back on the damp red bank

Had whales to catch

A hook to shank

Old cane pole firmly in my hand

Fishin' line tangled in a sweet grass stand

Grasshoppers playin' in wet red sand.

Bobble floats lazily

Dances hazily

Doing pirouettes on muddy water

Cottonmouth stretches

And a lark sings louder

Mud cat laughs

Catch me if you can

Ain't enough grease in your fryin' pan

A popcorn cloud

Circles high above

Me and this creek

We're just barefoot

Kids in love

Clouds
and
Clowns

Clouds and Clowns

It's so funny how clouds

And clowns are the same

You can turn that upside down

You know

While sitting on the sidewalk

In SoHo

Images floating by

Smilin', frowning faces that won't last

They come and go, up and down, so fast

First they're here, then they're passed

Rosy peaks and bulbous cheeks

Adorned with rouge and red

They could be clem, or could be fred

Mascara circled with Pacific hue

Surrounded with turquoise and light blue

Meeting us per chance

Clouds and clowns drenched in sun

Last Rose of Sharon

Last Rose of Sharon

The last Rose of Sharon

Holds tightly to the vine

Final days of sunset cast images sublime

Hues are thrown in quilted shades

While summer embers over horizons fade

Igniting, twinkling stars, contrasting black, that light.

Giving earth, 'neath moon, full flight

September's song comes to our ears

Summer's song serenading, fading . . .

Fall silently in stillness near

Find us short of breath, anticipating . . .

While the last Rose of Sharon

Lingers tightly on the vine

Her violet petals wide open

Kissed by summer's last sunshine

Leprechauns beneath her stalk

Expound!!! Upon a season's stalk

Sumac in the grove is red, betrothed to spring in summer
wed

While Rose of Sharon . . . last on the vine

Lays winter long upon my mind . . .

interruption

Interruption

On the rez

Just down the mountain from

Santa Fe de Chimayo

Where the paved road turns

Into chalky white dust of the pueblo

And a windmill whirls and

Dings in the breeze

Pumping sulfa-water and energy

Into a D/C battery that powers

An ice box and a

Single light bulb

We got radio

And you could hear it

I could not get away

Everywhere you could hear it

Finally, we got a TV.

It was turned on

And you could hear it.

Over the radio, you could hear it

I went into the back room

Closed the door tight

And you could hear it.

I turned the radio up

And you could hear it

My buddies and I

Got a bottle of tequila and went

Across the desert through the cactus and sage

To a mountain top

And you could hear it

So, we drank tequila and went

Higher into the mountains

Surrounded by pinion

And you could hear it.

So we drank more tequila and

Went to the top of the highest mountain

Where eagles launch themselves into flight

And you could still hear it.

After a while when we could not

Take it anymore

We came down and went across

The desert through the cactus and sage

And into the front room and

You could hear it

I pulled out my pistol

And I shot it.

And!!!

You can still hear it . . . .

Spiritual

Consciousness

Spiritual Consciousness

Spiritual consciousness

Open to thought

Body encased in conflict

From caverns locked inside

Within/without

Open to feeling

Eyes blinded by want

Open to sight

Darkness of the womb

Open to flight

When water touches

Flaming rock

Visions from darkness

Open to life

'neath willow encased trusses

Emanate poisons

Crusting mind and heart

Open

Life springs, illuminating

Earth, wind, fire, water

Touch the center

And bring together

Understanding

Human
Being

__Human Being__

Sitting on the front porch, dogs all around

Sunset approaches, night hawk cries

Longing cries

Still and silent

Remember the torch, ancient torch

Sun dance, blood flows

Lance, counted coup

Horse, spotted horse

Human being

Braids cascading over shoulders bronze

Entwined like bindweed over prairie

Move of the spider's web

Black and gray circled bed

Long and bound

Summer sun and winter wind embraced

Horizon sun—a song

Drums beat, pounding heart

Blood of the turtle, giant turtle

Human being

The mother enters slumber

With specks of stars

While moon heals inflicted scars

Chant now, songs of life and love

While spirit hawk circles

On endless wind above

Human being

Reverence

<u>Reverence</u>

We sat in the hot springs

Life songs, flute and drum sing

River, the child Rio,

Life's blood flows cold below

Through rocks of sacred Taos Peak

Visions we see, visions we seek

Like a phoenix, she rose from the water

Warm and tender,

Fair skin, hair black as cinder

Captured beads cascading down

Whippoorwill and river heart beating the only sound

Engulfed by starlight

She embraced mother night air's translucent ember

Kneeling

She basked in radiance

Grandmother smiles from above

Becoming one with moon and mother

Daughter stood, raised her arms

Became an eagle

Then a dove . . .

uncaged

<u>Uncaged</u>

The night air

Blows a got breath across black eons

My body is sweat entwined

With the essence of magnolia, honeysuckle, and mint.

In the light of a crescent moon

A cock crows at barking dogs down a dusty street

Imaginary shadows lurk

Behind a setting sun

While I peer through grease-stained windows

Images ignite in illumination

Reflecting broken prisms of faint moonlight

Down worn wooden stairs, a Bohemian mass stirs below

Auras casting blue in street light

Each hair crowned with a thousand stars

Blown from the blues man's horn

Melodic notes dance with a mantra

For the life of me, I can't remember

I press my body to the hot wet heat

Dress in madras and move to the street

Dragging up and down to a Cuban beat

I light a cigarette and cruise

Blowin' smoke on a sidewalk flush with clowns

Touchin' souls, dancin'

To a street vendor's sound

A soft breeze blows in from the gulf

Swirlin' halos in time

Bright eyes and bodies listin'

In the wind

A boat's horn blows low

Down the Ponchartrain

Erasing the dream and my vision

But look, see my tears

They fill the whole night sky

While the streets move like a carousel

In a calliope of sound

Painted puppets spin

On the puppeteer's strings, movin' round and round

And I hide behind a mask and stand

Refusing to face the mass

But I tap my button

And direct the band

It's Still
the
same

It's Still the Same

We were anarchists, we were idealists

My good friend, Green Camero John and I

Working days for enough cash

To go somewhere

I at a feedlot riding pens

John at a rendering plant south of town

At night we sat in a joint café

Behind a Fina station in a small west Texas town

Trapped, but looking for a way out

We drank rum straight, smuggled in;

In a brown paper bag, from greasy water glasses,

Listening to "Tea for the Tillerman" over and over

We talked philosophy, religion, politics

And we talked revolution

Of overthrowing the constricting lines of government

Of overthrowing constraining lines of society

Outside, diesel rigs roared down 287

Divided by a broken white line

South to El Paso, North to Colorado Springs

The sound of rubber and road keeping perfect time

With drowning engines until somewhere in the night

They made no sound in the disappearance

In the harmony of silence

Burned grease mingled with the smell of smoked opium

That rose from wooden benches in the alley out back

Waffling in through the kitchen screen door

On the spring night air

Until two a.m. we wrote a psychedelic dreams

Of mescaline things

Of worlds we were not part of

Nor could we ever be

Until Jose turned out the last lights

In town

And we walked through the night

Avoiding the local authority

While we waited for the diesel smoke

To take us to revolution

The smoke and the time came

And we went like moths to an open flame

And now no one is listening again.

Fear this "Revolution"

Fear this "Revolution"

How many bars

Can you place on your windows?

How many locks

Can you put on your door?

How many gated communities

Can you build for your safety

Concealing the faces of self-confined spirits?

Oh! How you sing the ode to security

How long can you sit, face blank,

In front of your TV?

Consuming volt after volt of virtual reality

You call it knowledge, you call it life

But it's really canned humanity

And each time a mustard seed of courage rises

The hand melts through the screen

To pour you another shot of fear

You can't run, you can't hide

Because you are your own terrorist

Following ta supremely appointed leader

Who fills his court with dangerous jesters?

Who draw their power from your plugged-in fear?

Yet sheep must be led by a Judas goat.

But do not despair too much

The wolf of emancipation screams across the land

It begins with a whisper—take a stand

It crescendos into a roar

Status quo begins to shake

Just listen!

It's revolution! Listen!

It's coming! Listen!

There is vision in revolution

There is strength in revolution

There is unity in revolution

There is power in revolution

There is—poetry in revolution

Old to Young -
Young to
Old

<u>Old to Young-Young to Old</u>

There was an old man

Walkin' down a dirt road

Dust risin' into the horizon from the dragging of his heels

Car broke down-It was an old car-

Been down this road many times before

Hair thin, face red, from a drink of cheap whiskey-

Clothes wrinkled and worn, stained from coffee spills-

With his old brown shoes

Scuffed, leather marred-

Heels worn, soles with holes,

He walked . . .

Kicked rocks and rusty beer cans into weedy bar ditches

Watched the dust settle, slowly,

Back into place . . .

He came upon a town, familiar, the journey . . .

Hopped a train—won't be back

But, will he remember . . .

There was a younger man

Walkin' down a dirt road

Car broke down—not such an old car

Dirt rose into the horizon from the pace of his step

Only been here a few times before

Clothes wearing, beginning to stain

Brown does barely scuffed

Kicked a rock, kicked a beer can

Saw only the imprint

He came upon a town, familiar . . .

Missed the train, won't remember

There was a young man

Walkin' down a dirt road

Car broke down, a new car, damn

Didn't see the dust, didn't see who's been there before

Didn't see the rocks or beer cans, didn't see the bar

ditches

Movin' too fast, no time today

Came upon a town

Train was in his way . . .

Where were they going?

Old to young-Young to old

Accepting

Dysfunction

<u>Accepting Dysfunction</u>

I really had no choice

I had to do it

After years of being

Sanitized . . . scrutinized . . . analyzed

Finally I have

Succumbed . . . surrendered . . . capitulated

I accept it!

I admit it!

I am dysfunctional

I am an . . . out of place . . . out of step . . .

Not quite right . . . unconformed . . . unintegrated . . .

Ph. D. in the absence of normalcy.

They have told me this . . . because

I like being . . .

Not on the line . . . by the line . . .

Straddling the line . . .

But just over there

On the other side of the line

That's drawn there by design

To fence me out

While it fences you in . . .

I like hair

Long, greasy hair

Slicked back tight with butch wax

Split ends blowing out of time

I like cars

Cars with fins

Flat fins and round fins

Low fins and high fins

Cars that sit close to the ground

With fender skirts and shiny chrome

Fussy dice and dingle balls

A dog on the back deck

Whose head goes round and round

I like sunsets

With colors of the rainbow

Splashed across the heavens

Where horizons begin

Where sunsets really never ends

It is merely the triumphant

Announcement of another sunrise

Orange puff balls

On opaque blue skies

Royal carpeting

For a waking sun

I like trains, late in the night

Heading in any direction

Like a long steel erection

Chugging toward anticipated eruption

Pausing at a momentary emotional destination

And, I like gang bangs

Where the woman on the bottom

Is placed upon a pedestal

And as the night turns into day

A temple is raised

In hushed and reverent voices

Her name is announced with deities

Venus, Helen, Aphrodite

I like arbors

Brush arbors . . . singing "Bringing in the Sheaves"

Preaching hellfire and brimstone

A man, brother . . . how great thou art

Down by the riverside

With Jesus, the bugs and ticks and fleas

Upon further reflection

I ask the question

Is it possible

That I can be all of these

Well of course I can be

I am dysfunctional, you see

Don't you understand

That assimilation to the

Social quagmire of accepted association

Is nothing more than castration

And that if you still have

Your heart, soul, or your mind

It's OK

You could be dysfunctional too

And it's alright

If the dance you do

And the song you sing

Is out of step or way out of tune.

Alphabet Soup:

LDDS-ADDS-ADHD-LSD
OR
This Ain't Walt Whitman

Alphabet Soup:

LDDS-ADDS-ADHD-LSD

OR

This Ain't Walt Whitman

Once upon a time

In a land that giants maligned

Great Philistines

Inhibited by

One-eyed Fred and Jack the dread

A wise man, well-read, once said

There was and there was

The list

The Beat

The Hip

The X generation . . .

Out of place children

Who did not fit, alteration

Sew up the seams

Of adolescent wet dreams

Desolate minds, abandon, deserted isolation

Wooly mammoth dredge

Drawn hide . . . encrusted stand

Across eons . . . eons

Wallowing in the mire

Sweaty, dirty, hair balls

Dangles attached to each strand

Ivory tusk extraction

Massive holes ripped! By saber tooth

Blood extracted.

Corporate social laceration

Dripping, pouring into pools of human coagulation

Eyes red, road map, deluge

Pourin' down rain

Wind gust dry

Can't cry, brain on fry!

Can't weep open wound

Town ripped, soul deep,

From cracked cocoon

Scurrying to fit inside the lines

Humanity closes the blinds

Venetian blinds

Drawn tight, dark charcoal lines

Pulled shut

By the man in the mask

Behind a curtain, velvet lines

Uncertain knowledge from a subliminal flask

Comes now!

A new generation

Re-birth exultation

Whose child do we find

Tell me, tell us, tell the world the rag

Put a label on it, children

You're it . . . Tag!!!

Faces pale, eyes blank

Small hands clinched in a fist

On sidewalks straight-lined you list

To and fro

Slurping from the swill

Behavior not taught

Vision not sought

Canaan's last, masses lost

Wandering in the desert of compulsive consumption

Just one inalienable right

You Ratalin lads and lasses

Mass assumption

Consume! Consume!

More and more and more

Until you burst . . .

Oozing eruption

Ebbing tidal waves of hysteria

Emasculated by pills at a pharmaceutical through

Ingested, injected

Be calm, be quiet inflicted

Analyzed, sanitized, corporationalized

To fit . . . .

Not realized, just computed shit

Sitting, standing, gazing, searching, lost . . .

Gun at head . . . hammer cocked . . .

And! We're surprised they've quit

Except for the scream

A nightmare's dream

Flash of light! . . . Clasp of thunder

Blunder, Blunder, Blunder

Throw out the lifeline, blunderbuss

Teeter-totter, bread and water

We've pushed the child under

Mother; oh mother!

Don't weep for son or daughter

Armour meat is fun to eat

Just press the cash, flash the card.

Love, love, love

Their life is such a breeze

With a corporate logo on their sleeve . . .

Woman with Cat Eyes

Woman with Cat Eyes

Woman with cat eyes

The sustenance of eternity;

Exceeds binding chains of humanity.

Emerald green touched by aqua blue

Splashed with sparklets

A halo's golden hue

Tangled locks

Black hair flowing

Soft silk over shoulders of ebony.

Cascading to enhance

Soft wind blowing

Primitive breast protruding

Casting off chastity

The dun sifts long rays through; clarity

Translucent cloth

Bare arms to hands

Thighs parted welcome

Beckon, beckon

Aphrodite calls

Oh! Waif of salt and sand

What shall these pools reflect

Loins silhouetted in bright sunlight

Radiance blossoms

Helen's mound entices and invites

Hector guards no heat more intense

Levity . . . and larks in full flight

Yet Achilles stalks

A panther to pounce

Salivating—primal instincts

Passion stifled

Nears the brink

Ignited by the fragrance of lust

Venus induces Sun to rise

Claps his mouth and utters beauty

In a silent hush

Fires are kindled as

Poppies spread their counterpane

And daisies make a pillow

She heard

Before devoured . . .

Visions drink luscious heads

Nectar from a flowing well

While ears hear poems

No lyre can tell

But the eyes are azure blue

A touch of yellow

A halo's hue

Residence of

<u>Residence of</u>

Re-write when you're ab-normal

Take your tie off, trash the façade

Remove the mask

Don't be so freakin' formal

Somewhere on the page

See!!!

You and I are the caged

See!!!

Playin' with our pee pees

See!!!

Suchin' our thumbs to entertain society

See!!!

While spreadin' our cheeks, to enlighten

The gilded corset,

Encased in emeralds and rubies

And the blood and bones of humanity

Learning genetically, biologically, inherently,

That we ourselves!!!

Keep the cage of reality

Unless we go

To and fro

Hither-thither-and you

"itsy-bitsy-spider"

In pale patterns of Gauguin's Dawn

But!!!

Someone comes from behind

Sneakin' up to find

That you and I

Up and down

Cannot be found

'twixr or 'tween

Unless they can see

Somewhere half-between

The world of men

And make believe

Let
sleeping
Giants
Lie

Let Sleeping Giants Lie

The giant sleeps

Controller of all action, thought and art

Safe in his complacency and contempt

While trolls guard

The borders of his coffers

Criminals patrol his streets

Insuring his laws we keep

Don't wake him

Don't shake him

Let the giant slumber

Sweet dreams

Of shackles, chains, and golden geese

The invasion long past

Begins again

Dancing on his star bed

Silently wrinkling the satin sheets

Don't wake him

Don't shake him

Let the giant slumber

When he awakes

The piñata breaks

He'll be insane

Too late

Now anarchy hold the reins

Red Dress

Revolution

Red Dress Revolution

Spanish guitars strum slowly, melody lifts

Gleaming stars bright like a sieve

Through faces powdered, painted sifts

Red dress upward flies

I see your thighs

To heights unseen adorn

Free as pollen on air we're born

Leaves us to bleached bone, bare

Brave souls to dare

Makes men to rise

Makes battle cries

Sabers and saddles crack and creak

All are so bravely weak

Oh, come country man low and high

Hear now you heed the cry

There's gold for you if you will stand

'neath banners high golden eagles fly

Tequila come to me

There are sights that I must see

Worm's hot meat

We all shall eat

Worm turns and greets its host

While bourgeois castles toast

Before fire, wine and quail

Sending common man to fail

Tequila come to me

Stale breath, that I might see

Earthly eternity.

Spanish guitars strum slowly

Melody lifts, blank faces sift

Through fading stars to back-street bars

Red dress flies

Above your thighs

Anarchy screams, then weeps and cries

Now! Now! Classes die . . . consumed . . .

Engulfed by sweet perfume

Revolution, distribution,

Resolution.

Come out, come out, come out

And play

Those who enslave

With gold must pay

As with those who've given all

Upon their gilded swords will fall

Bugles call the gun, ground quakes

While all the emerald cities shake . . .

Red dress dancing flies

I see your thighs

To heights unseen adorn

We all as one are born

Spanish guitars strum

Revolution-

Circles

Circles

Night is now quiet

Wind that howled all day

Has lain still

Grandmother moon adorned in radiance

Rises in splendor

Through bows and arms of leafless blackjack and crusted

red cedar

Lightly brightly divided by thistles beaming

Like the headlight of a fast-moving freight

Moonbeams cast magic shadows

Through spider webs

That cling tightly to tumbleweeds

Blown across the tracks

By the day's winds.